Published by
Lion Hudson Limited
Wilkinson House, Jordan Hill Business Park
Banbury Road, Oxford OX2 8DR, England
www.lionhudson.com

ISBN 978 0 7459 7795 9

First edition 2020

A catalogue record for this book is available from the British Library

Printed and bound in Malaysia, February 2020, LH54

Albert and the Good Sister

The Story of Moses in the Bulrushes

Written by Richard Littledale

Illustrated by Heather Heyworth

LION CHILDREN'S

"Psst," came a little squeaky voice as Albert lay dozing in a shady corner.

Albert peered down his nose to see a tiny nut-brown harvest mouse looking up at him.

"Can I ask you a question?" she squeaked. He nodded, and she went on. "I am the smallest mouse in the whole field. I have six brothers and every single one is bigger than me. They say I'm just a silly mouselet and I'll never be any use. Is it true?"

Albert made space for her just inside the curl of his tail, and began to tell a story. His very-very-great-aunt Lapis, who once lived in Egypt, had told it to him.

"Lapis lived in a tiny nest near a big river in Egypt, the River Nile. In the house nearby, there were two children, Miriam and Moses. Lapis kept a careful eye on both of them wherever they went.

"Miriam was a big sister to her baby brother, Moses. One day Moses would have a great big voice, like a tiger roaring. Not now, though. Now, he was small, chubby, and gurgly, like most babies.

“Early one morning, Lapis was munching on a crumb of bread when she overheard Miriam speaking to her mother. Her mother was packing Moses into a basket.

“‘Why are you doing that?’ Miriam asked.

"'To keep him safe,' Miriam's mother said. 'Mighty Pharaoh has said that he hates all our baby boys, and he will surely kill them if he gets the chance.'

"In her hiding place, Lapis put her nose in her paws. She hated the sound of that.

"The basket had special tar painted on the bottom to make it waterproof, and some soft blankets inside for baby Moses.

“Before the mother picked up the basket, she knelt down before Miriam, and placed her hand on the girl’s shoulder.

“‘Do you remember the day Moses was born, and I asked you to be a good big sister to him?’ she asked.

“Miriam nodded.

“‘Well today, I want you to remember that,’ said her mother.

“Miriam went with her mother down to the River Nile, and watched as she nudged the little basket into the reeds. As her mother went back home, Miriam stayed to watch from where she hid.

“Behind Miriam, in the shade of a specially tall reed, Lapis was hiding. She had followed them.

"The sun climbed higher and higher in the sky and Miriam was very thirsty, but she didn't move. Up above, great white egrets flapped across the sky, but Miriam did not move. Sometimes a strange movement made the waters ripple. Was it a crocodile? But she did not move.

"Lapis did not move either. She was so thirsty and so hot, but she wouldn't leave Miriam and her baby brother all alone.

"Hours later, Lapis pricked up her teeny tiny ears as she heard footsteps coming closer. Living so close to the ground, she knew how everybody's feet sounded. These were the feet of strangers.

"Sure enough, a beautiful lady and her maid came by. The lady was the Princess, Pharaoh's daughter. She and her maid pulled the basket out of the reeds and peered in. They both cried, 'Ah!' as they looked down at the little baby.

“Taking a very deep breath, Miriam stepped forward. She had never spoken to a princess before.

‘Shall I find someone to look after the baby for you, Your Highness?’

“The princess nodded. ‘Go and find someone who can look after the baby for me,’ she said.

"Miriam knew the very best person in the whole world to take care of her baby brother. As she ran home, nobody saw the tiny tail and the speedy paws of a little mouse running beside her.

"Grasping her mother's hand, Miriam brought her to meet the princess.

“As her maid handed over the basket with baby Moses inside, the princess explained that she would like him to be cared for until he was old enough to go and live at the palace.

“Lapis pricked up her ears at the mention of a palace. She wondered what sort of crumbs she might find on the floor there. She wouldn’t go though – she belonged with the people who needed her.

"As the princess turned to leave, Moses' mother looked back over her shoulder and winked at Miriam.

"Miriam had kept her word. She had been a good sister to Moses. Sometimes, watching out for another person is the most important job of all, and you don't have to be big to do it."

Albert looked down to see if the tiny harvest mouse was still listening, but she was already wriggling free.

"Sorry," she said. "I have an important job to do. Someone needs *me* to watch over them." With that, she was gone.

Albert went back to sleep,
dreaming of his tiny very-very-great-aunt Lapis.